Home Canning Uncovered

A Culinary Adventure in Canning Fruits, Vegetables, Jellies, Jams, Pickles, Meats and More. Transform Your Kitchen into a Flavor Haven

Julia M. Moody

2 | JULIA M. MOODY

TABLE OF CONTENTS

Introduction to Canning Preservation 8

History and Benefits 8

Types of Canning (Water Bath, Pressure Canning) 10

Basic Principles of Food Safety 16

Equipment and Supplies 20

Essential Tools and Equipment 20

Choosing the Right Jars and Lids 25

Other Supplies (Funnels, Ladles, etc.) 29

Ingredients and Preparation 34

Selecting Fresh Produce 34

Preparing Fruits, Vegetables, Meats 37

Sugar, Salt, and Acid in Canning 41

Step-by-Step Canning Processes 47

Water Bath Canning 47

Pressure Canning 50

Troubleshooting Common Issues 55

Recipes for Beginners 62

Simple Jams and Jellies 62

Strawberry Jam 62

Blueberry Jelly 63

Apple Jelly 65

Pickles and Relishes 66

Classic Dill Pickles 66

Sweet Pickle Relish 68

Spicy Pickled Jalapeños. 70

Tomato-Based Products 72

Homemade Tomato Sauce 72

Tomato Salsa 74

Tomato paste 76

Advanced Canning Recipes 79

Preserving Meats and Poultry 79

Canning Beef Stew 79

Canning Chicken 81

Canning Pork Tenderloin 82

Canned chicken broth: 84

Canning Soups and Stews 86

Beef and Vegetable Stew 86

Chicken and Rice Soup 88

Tomato-based Minestrone Soup 90

Complex Sauces and Condiments 92

Homemade Barbecue Sauce 92

Spicy Salsa Verde. 94

Gourmet Mustard 95

Pickled hot peppers. 97

Seasonal and Regional Recipes 99

Canning with Seasonal Produce 99

Spring Asparagus Spears 99

Summer Tomato Sauce 100

Fall Pumpkin Butter 102

Winter Root Vegetable Pickle 104

Regional Specialties Across the United States 106

Southern Pickled Okra 106

New England Baked Beans 108

Midwestern Sweet Corn Relish 109

Southwest Salsa 111

Storage and Shelf Life 114

Proper Storage Conditions 114

Understanding Shelf Life 116

Signs of Spoilage 119

Creative Uses for Preserved Foods 124

Recipes Incorporating Canned Goods 124

Canned Tomato Basil Soup. 124

Canned Green Bean Casserole. 126

Canned peach crisp. 127

Canned beef stew. 128

Gifting and Sharing Canned Foods 130

Crafting with Canning Jars 133

INTRODUCTION TO CANNING PRESERVATION

History and Benefits

Canning has a remarkable history, dating back to the early nineteenth century.

Here's a quick overview:

Canning's origins can be traced back to the late 18th century when it was used to preserve food for extended durations. In 1795, the French government announced a prize for developing a way of preserving food for its soldiers. Nicolas Appert, a French chef, earned the award for his method of sealing food in glass jars and heating it to eliminate microorganisms.

Canning Technology Development: In 1810, a British businessman named Peter Durand invented metal cans, further perfecting the canning technique. His method entailed storing food in tin-plated iron cans, which were more robust and portable than glass jars.

Canning technology went to the United States and quickly gained popularity. Commercial canning facilities were built by the mid-nineteenth century, and the technology became widely used to preserve fruits, vegetables, and meats.

Modern Advances: Canning technology has evolved throughout time. Pressure canning, as well as improved canning lids and seals, have enhanced the process's reliability and accessibility to home canners.

Benefits of Canning

Canning has various advantages that make it a popular technique for preserving food.

- **Long Shelf Life:** Canning extends food's shelf life, allowing you to keep it for months or even years without refrigeration. This is particularly handy for storing seasonal crops.
- **Nutrient Retention:** Properly canned foods maintain a significant portion of their nutritious content. This means you can eat fruits and vegetables out of season while still getting many of the vitamins and minerals they contain.

- **Cost-effective:** Canning can be less expensive than purchasing commercially canned foods, especially if you raise your produce or buy in quantity at a discounted price. Canning reduces food waste by preserving extra produce. It's a terrific method to finish off fruits and veggies before they spoil.
- **Customization:** Home canning lets you change the flavors, modify the sugar and salt levels, and avoid preservatives present in store-bought products. This can be especially tempting to people with dietary limitations or preferences.

Canning is often regarded as a pleasant hobby. It can also be a chance to reconnect with family traditions and heritage, as canning has been practiced in many countries for millennia.

Types of Canning (Water Bath, Pressure Canning)

Canning can be broadly divided into two types: water bath canning and pressure canning. Each method is appropriate for different sorts of food and requires its own set of guidelines and equipment.

Water Bath Canning

- **Overview:** Water bath canning, often called boiling water canning, is a technique for preserving high-acid foods. The method is immersing food jars in boiling water for a set period to kill bacteria, yeasts, and molds that could cause deterioration.

Suitable Foods:

Fruits (such as peaches, apples, and berries)

Fruit juices

Pickles and pickled veggies.

Tomatoes (acidified or in recipes with additional acids such as lemon juice or vinegar)

Jams, jelly, and preserves.

Equipment Required:

Water bath canner (big pot with a rack or deep stockpot)

Canning jars have two-piece lids (jars and bands).

Jar lifter

Canning funnel

Bubble removal and headspace tool

Procedure:

Wash and sterilize the jars and lids.

Fill the jars with prepared food, leaving the recommended headspace.

Wipe the jar rims to remove any residue.

Screw on the jar lids and bands until fingertip tight.

Submerge the jars in a canner filled with boiling water, making sure the water covers them by at least 1 inch.

Process the jars for the time indicated in the recipe.

After processing, remove the jars and let them cool on a clean cloth or cooling rack.

Key points:

Water bath canning is appropriate for foods with high acidity since boiling water can reach temperatures high enough to kill most bacteria and molds.

To ensure safety, always use well-tested recipes and processing timeframes.

Pressure canning.

- **Overview:** Pressure canning is used to preserve low-acid foods. This method uses a pressure canner to attain greater temperatures than boiling water alone, which is required to kill botulinum spores and other hazardous microorganisms.

Suitable Foods:

Vegetables (such as green beans, corn and carrots)

Meat and poultry.

Seafood

Soups and Stews

Broths

Equipment Required:

Pressure canner (a heavy-duty pot with a locking top and a pressure gauge or weight).

Canning jars have two-piece lids.

Jar lifter

Canning funnel

Bubble removal and headspace tool

Procedure:

Wash and sterilize the jars and lids.

Fill the jars with prepared food, leaving the recommended headspace.

Wipe the jar rims to remove any residue.

Screw on the jar lids and bands until fingertip tight.

Place the jars in the pressure canner and add water according to the manufacturer's instructions.

Lock the lid and heat until the canner achieves the desired pressure.

Process the jars for the period stated in the recipe, keeping the pressure constant.

After processing, turn off the heat and let the canner cool and depressurize before opening.

Remove the jars and let them cool on a clean towel or cooling rack.

Key points:

Pressure canning is required for low-acid foods to reduce the danger of botulism.

To maintain proper pressure levels, utilize a pressure canner equipped with a dependable gauge or weight.

To maintain food safety, always use tested recipes and processing timeframes.

Basic Principles of Food Safety

Ensuring food safety during the canning process is critical for preventing spoilage and foodborne illness. Here are the essential guidelines for food safety to follow while canning:

Use Tested Recipes: Ensure recipes are safe and reliable. Tested recipes ensure that the processing periods and methods are successful in destroying hazardous microorganisms and preserving food securely.

Proper sterilization and preparation.

- **Jars and lids:** To prevent bacteria and mold growth, sterilize jars and lids before use. Wash jars in hot, soapy water, then sterilize them by boiling for 10 minutes or putting them in a hot dishwasher. Lids should be simmered (not boiled) in boiling water right before use.
- **Food Preparation:** Before canning, make sure that the food is clean and thoroughly prepared. Wash the fruits and vegetables well, and remove any damaged or bruised portions.

Use the Right Equipment.

- **Jars:** Make sure to use canning jars. Do not use old or repurposed jars that were not intended for canning because they may not seal correctly or resist heat.
- **Lids and Bands:** Use a fresh lid for each canning process. While bands can be reused in good condition, they should be checked for corrosion and distortion.

Follow the Headspace Guidelines.

Leave the required quantity of headspace (the space between the top of the food and the jar rim) as mentioned in the recipe. Headspace is essential for ensuring a proper seal and allowing the food to expand during processing.

Ensure proper sealing.

- **Sealing:** Make sure the lid is firmly sealed by looking for a concave center and an even gap around the edges. A properly sealed jar will not move when pressed in the center of the lid.

Monitor processing times and temperatures.

- **Processing Times:** Use the precise processing times specified in proven recipes. Process timings are calculated to guarantee that dangerous microorganisms are eliminated.
- **Temperatures:** For water bath canning, keep the water at a rolling boil throughout the entire time. For pressure canning, follow the directions for achieving and maintaining the proper pressure.

Avoid cross-contamination.

- **Cleanliness:** Keep your work surfaces, utensils, and hands clean to avoid introducing bacteria into the jars. Avoid touching the inside rims of jars and lids with your hands.
- **Store canned foods:** Proper storage conditions include keeping canned foods cool, dark, and dry. Ideal storage temperatures range from 50°F to 70°F (10°C to 21°C) with minimal humidity.
- **Shelf Life:** To ensure the highest quality, use canned items within the prescribed time limit. While

properly preserved foods can last for years, they are best consumed within one to two years.

Inspect Jars Before Use

- **Visual Inspection:** Before using canned food, look for symptoms of decomposition such as bulging lids, unpleasant odors, or strange colors. If a jar appears to be tampered with or if the seal is broken, dump the contents.

Practice good personal hygiene.

Wash your hands properly before and during the canning process to avoid contamination.

Wear clean clothing and avoid touching your face or hair while working with food and jars.

By following these basic guidelines, you may ensure that your home-canned items are safe, nutritious, and fun to consume.

EQUIPMENT AND SUPPLIES

Essential Tools and Equipment

Canning Jars

- **Description:** Glass jars used for canning. They come in a variety of sizes and forms.
- **Use:** Ideal for storing preserved foods. Ensure that the jars are in good shape, with no cracks or chips.

Canning Lids:

Description: Metal or composite lids with sealing compound on the underside. They come with an additional metal band or ring.

Use: The lids create an airtight seal on the jars. To guarantee a proper seal, always use new lids when canning.

Canning Bands (Rings):

- **Description:** Metal rings screw onto jars to keep lids in place during processing.
- **Use:** In conjunction with lids. Bands can be reused provided they are not corroded or broken.

Canning Pot (Water Bath Canner)

- **Description:** A large pot with a rack or perforated insert for jars. It should be tall enough to hold at least **an inch of water above the jars.**
- **Use:** For water bath canning of high-acid foods.

Pressure Canner:

- **Description:** A heavy-duty pot with a locking cover, pressure gauge, weight, and rack. It is designed to withstand the higher temperatures required for processing low-acid meals.
- **Use:** Pressure canning destroys bacteria and prevents botulism.

Jar Lifter:

- **Description:** A tool with a spring-loaded grip for safely lifting hot jars from the canner.
- **Use:** Prevents burns and makes it easier to handle jars.

Canning Funnel:

- **Description:** A wide-mouthed funnel designed to prevent spills when pouring food into jars.
- **Use:** It makes filling jars easier and cleaner.

Bubble Removal and Headspace Tool

- **Description:** A tool with a flat edge for removing air bubbles and a built-in headspace indicator.
- **Use:** Maintains proper headspace and eliminates air bubbles that could compromise the seal.

Lid Wand (Magnetic Lid Lifter):

- **Description:** A little magnetic gadget for lifting canning lids from hot water.
- **Use:** Allows you to place lids on jars without contaminating the sealing surface.

Kitchen timer for tracking jar processing time.

- **Use:** Ensures that jars are treated for the appropriate period.

Optional Tools.

Canning Rack

- **Description:** A metal rack that fits into the canning pot to keep jars off the bottom and enable water to flow.
- **Use:** Prevents jars from touching the pot's bottom, which might lead to breakage.

Jar Brush

- **Description:** A brush for cleaning the inside of jars.
- **Use:** Clean jars thoroughly before use.

Food Processor

- **Description:** A kitchen appliance that chops, slices, and blends.
- **Use:** Ideal for prepping fruits and vegetables for canning.

Funnel with Wide Mouth.

- **Description:** A funnel has a bigger mouth to fill jars with larger items.
- **Use:** Makes it easier to fill jars with large goods or combinations.

Canning Labels

Stickers or tags to label jars.

- **Use:** For keeping track of material and processing dates.

Storage containers

- **Description:** Containers used to store canning supplies and ingredients.
- **Use:** Keeps everything organized and ready to use.

These tools and equipment will allow you to preserve your food effectively and safely.

Choosing the Right Jars and Lids

Choosing the correct jars and lids is critical to the safety and effectiveness of your canning operation. Here's what you should know.

Types of Jars.

Mason jars are the most frequent form of container used for home canning. Available in both conventional and wide-mouth variants.

Regular Mouth Jars: These jars have a narrower opening and are better suited for smaller goods like jams and jelly.

Wide-mouth jars have a larger opening, making them easier to fill and clean. They are perfect for larger products, such as whole fruits and vegetables.

Sizes

Pint Jars (16 oz) are ideal for jams, sauces, and small amounts of fruit or vegetables.

Quart Jars (32 oz): Ideal for storing bigger amounts of food, such as pickles, tomatoes, and meat.

Half-gallon jars (64 oz) are commonly used for bulk storage of products such as pickles or juices.

Material

Glass jars are preferred for canning due to their no reactivity and ability to endure high temperatures. Always use canning jars.

Avoid Using:

- **Reused Jars:** Do not use jars that are not specifically designed for canning (for example, jars from store-bought food), since they may not seal correctly or endure the canning process.
- **Damaged Jars:** Discard any jars that have cracks or chips, as they may not seal correctly and break during processing.

Condition

Before using jars, inspect them for evidence of breakage or defects.

Cleaning: Before using the jars, wash them in hot, soapy water. Sterilize as directed per the recipe.

Types of Lids.

- **Two-Piece Lids:** Made out of a flat metal lid with a sealing compound and a separate metal band (ring). This is the most frequent variety used for home canning.
- **One-piece Lids:** These are typically used for industrial canning and are not recommended for home canning due to the lack of seal integrity compared to two-piece lids.

Selecting Lids

Use new lids for each canning operation. Reusing lids is not suggested since the sealing substance may be weakened, resulting in faulty sealing.

Lid Quality: Choose lids from reputed manufacturers to ensure high-quality materials and a reliable seal.

Preparing lids

- **Preparation:** Before using two-piece lids, place the flat lids in hot water and simmer (not boil) them. This softens the sealing substance, allowing for a better seal. Avoid overheating, as this can harm the sealing compound.
- **Avoid Pre-Heating:** Do not preheat or boil one-piece lids, since this might cause damage.

Sealing and Storing Lids

- **Check Seals:** After processing, press the center of each lid to check the seal. If the lid is concave and does not move, the seal is probably intact.
- **Storage:** Keep unused lids cold and dry, away from moisture and sunshine. Keep them in the original package to prevent damage.

Common Issues

- **Failure to Seal:** If a lid does not seal properly, refrigerate the jar and use it within a few days. The meal can be reprocessed with a new lid if necessary, or it can be consumed immediately.

- **Buckling:** If the lid becomes buckled or uneven during processing, the seal may be compromised. Check that the jars are properly processed, and adhere to the recipe's headspace and processing time restrictions.

You can assure the safety and effectiveness of your canning operation by choosing the right jars and lids and carefully prepping them.

Other Supplies (Funnels, Ladles, etc.)

In addition to jars and lids, having the correct additional supplies can help the canning process run more smoothly and efficiently. Here's a list of useful canning equipment and supplies:

Funnels: A wide-mouthed funnel that fits into jars and prevents spilling.

- **Use:** Makes filling jars easy and decreases the possibility of spillage or mess.

Ladles: A big, deep spoon with a long handle used to scoop and ladle hot liquids or foods into jars.

- **Use:** Allows for the safe and efficient transfer of hot meals or liquids from pots to jars.

Jar Lifters: A tool with spring-loaded grips used to remove hot jars from the canner without contacting the boiling water.

- **Use:** Promotes safe jar handling and prevents burns.

Bubble Remover and Headspace Tool: This tool features a flat edge for removing air bubbles from jars and a built-in meter for evaluating headspace.

- **Use:** Maintains proper headspace and eliminates trapped air bubbles that could compromise the seal.

Lid Wand (Magnetic Lid Lifter): A little magnetic gadget for lifting hot canning lids from pots of hot water.

- **Use:** Allows you to place lids on jars without contaminating the sealing surface.

Canning Rack: A metal rack that fits inside the canner to elevate jars and improve water circulation.

- **Use:** Prevents jars from touching the bottom of the canner, which can lead to breakage.

Jar Brush: A brush used to clean the inside of jars.

- **Use:** Clean jars well before use to remove any residues or particles.

Canning Labels: Stickers or tags used to label jars with contents and processing dates.

- **Use:** Keeps track of what is in each jar and when it was processed.

Timer: A kitchen timer for tracking jar processing time.

- **Use:** Ensures that jars are processed for the appropriate amount of time, ensuring safety and preservation.

Storage Containers: Used for storing canning supplies like jars, lids, and equipment.

- **Use:** Keep your canning supplies organized and ready to use.

Food Processors or Blenders: Kitchen appliances used to chop, slice, and blend fruits and vegetables.

- **Use:** Ideal for prepping items before canning, particularly for sauces, purees, and finely chopped dishes.

Pot Holders or Oven Mitts: Handle hot canning equipment safely with these protective gloves or pads.

- **Use:** Keeps your hands safe from burns while handling hot jars, lids, or the canner itself.

Thermometer: A tool for measuring the interior temperature of food or boiling water.

Use: Make sure the water bath or pressure canner reaches and maintains the proper temperature for safe canning.

Keeping these supplies on hand will assist in streamlining the canning process and guarantee that it is completed safely and efficiently.

33 | JULIA M. MOODY

INGREDIENTS AND PREPARATION

Selecting Fresh Produce

Selecting the appropriate produce is critical for effective canning. Here's how to choose fresh fruits and veggies.

Quality and ripeness

- **Ripeness:** Select fruits and vegetables that are completely ripe but not overripe. Overripe produce may already be started to rot, compromising the taste and safety of your canned goods.
- **Firmness:** Select food that feels firm to the touch. Soft or mushy patches may indicate spoilage or decay, which can lower the overall quality of your canned goods.

Appearance

- **Visual inspection:** Look for fruits and vegetables with brilliant colors and no blemishes, bruises, or cuts. Damaged vegetables can lead to spoiling and reduce the quality of canned meals.

- **Uniformity:** Select produce that is consistent in size and shape to ensure even processing and cooking.
- **Recommended Variety:** Choose canning-friendly types. Some fruit, such as tomato varietals or pickling cucumbers, is specifically cultivated to be canned and preserved.
- **Purpose-Specific types:** Choose types that are appropriate for their intended application, such as jams, pickles, sauces, or simply preserved fruits and vegetables.

Freshness.

- **Timing:** Consume produce as soon as possible following purchase or harvest. The longer produce sits, the more its quality degrades, harming the finished canned product.
- **Storage:** If you can't process the vegetables right away, keep them in a cold, dry area to prevent deterioration. Refrigeration can help preserve freshness, although it is not always necessary.

Size and Weight:

- **Size:** Select vegetables based on jar size and recipe requirements. Larger things may require different cuts or preparations to fit inside jars.
- **Weight:** Heavier food is more suited for canning since it is more flavorful and has a better texture after processing.

Seasonality

- **Seasonal Produce:** Choose fruits and vegetables that are in season for the best flavor and value. Seasonal produce is usually fresher and less expensive.
- **Local Resources:** Consider buying from local farmers' markets or farms to receive the freshest produce while also supporting local agriculture.

Selecting high-quality, fresh vegetables is critical for getting the greatest outcomes from your canning efforts. Proper ingredient selection ensures that your preserved goods are flavorful and safe for long-term storage.

Preparing Fruits, Vegetables, Meats

Fruit Washing:

Rinse fruits thoroughly with cold water to remove dirt, pesticides, and residues. Use a brush for fruits with rough skins.

Peeling and coring:

- **Peeling:** Use a vegetable peeler or knife to peel fruits, such as apples or peaches, as directed in the recipe.
- **Coring:** Remove the cores from fruits such as apples and pears. Use a corer or knife to remove all inedible portions.

Cutting and slicing:

- **Size:** Cut fruits into uniform pieces to ensure equal cooking and simpler packaging into jars. For particular size measurements, refer to the recipe directions.

- **Slicing:** Depending on the desired size and recipe requirements cut fruits like peaches and apricots in **half or quarters.**

Blanching (if necessary):

Some fruits, such as peaches, benefit from blanching to loosen the skins and keep the color. Blanch in boiling water for a few minutes before transferring to icy water.

Adding acid:

Add lemon juice or ascorbic acid to avoid browning and keep color, especially for fruits that oxidize quickly.

Vegetable Washing:

Rinse veggies with cold water to remove soil and residues. Use a brush to clean root vegetables such as carrots and potatoes.

Peeling and trimming:

Peel veggies as needed, such as potatoes or carrots. Use a knife or vegetable peeler.

Trimming involves removing any damaged or tough components, such as stems and leaves. Trim to ensure uniformity in the components.

Cutting:

- **Size:** Cut vegetables into uniform pieces following the recipe. This enables even cooking and correct packing in the jars.

Blanching:

Blanch veggies by briefly boiling them and then placing them in icy water. This helps to preserve color, flavor, and texture. Follow particular timeframes for each veggie.

Cooling and Drainage:

After blanching, chill the vegetables rapidly and completely. Drain thoroughly to eliminate any excess water before packing into jars.

Meats Selection and Preparation:

Select fresh, high-quality meats. Trim away any excess fat or gristle, as fat can go rancid over time and degrade the quality of canned meat.

Cutting and cubing:

Cut the meat into consistent cubes or bits, as directed in the recipe. This aids in even cooking and packing.

Pre-cooking (if applicable):

Some recipes call for precooking or browning meat before canning. This procedure improves texture and flavor.

Packing:

Pack the meat into jars, leaving the necessary headspace as described in the recipe. If desired, season with salt and pepper or use broth.

Processing:

Follow the recipe's instructions for processing time and pressure. This guarantees that the meat is completely cooked and properly preserved.

Proper preparation of fruits, vegetables, and meats is required for successful canning. Following these steps will guarantee that your ingredients are ready for safe and effective storage.

Sugar, Salt, and Acid in Canning

Sugar Purpose:

Sugar improves the flavor and sweetness of fruits and preserves, making the result more appealing.

Sugar preserves the texture and color of fruits by absorbing moisture and limiting bacterial growth.

Types:

Granulated sugar is commonly used in jams, jelly, and fruit preserves.

Brown sugar has a unique flavor profile and can be utilized in dishes such as baked products and some pickles.

Alternative sweeteners include honey and maple syrup, but quantities should be adjusted and specific recipe instructions followed.

Usage:

- **Amount:** Carefully follow the sugar quantity specified in the recipe. Too much sugar can alter the texture and consistency, while too little can cause spoiling.
- **Adjustments:** If you use less sugar, consider how it may affect the finished result. Some recipes may require modifications to acidity or processing times.

Salt Purpose:

Salt improves the flavor of canned vegetables, meats, and pickles.

Preservation: Salt draws moisture out of pickled items and inhibits bacterial growth.

Types:

Canning Salt: This salt is ideal for canning since it is pure and free of additives that can cloud brines or alter food texture.

Kosher salt can be used, however it adds bulk and may influence brine concentration. If using, take careful measurements.

Table salt is not advised for canning since it contains anti-caking chemicals, which can compromise brine clarity and canned goods quality.

Usage:

- **Amount:** Use the salt quantity specified in the recipe. Excess salt can make food overly salty, but too little might affect preservation and flavor.
- **Adjustments:** For nutritional reasons, reduce or omit salt; however, keep in mind that this may influence flavor and preservation. Adjust the other ingredients or processing times as needed.

Acid Purpose:

Safety: Acid helps to establish an environment that prevents the growth of hazardous bacteria, including Clostridium botulinum, which can cause botulism.

Acid preserves the color, texture, and flavor of fruits and vegetables.

Types:

Vinegar is commonly used in pickling and in recipes that require acidity. Use white vinegar or apple cider vinegar with a 5% acid content.

Lemon juice: A natural source of acidity that is commonly utilized in fruit preserves and tomato-based dishes. Bottled lemon juice provides consistent acidity.

Citric Acid: A pure acid used to alter the acidity level in recipes, particularly when canning low-acid foods such as tomatoes.

Usage:

- **Amount:** Ensure that the acid requirements in the recipe are met precisely. Inadequate acid might result in dangerous canned items, but excessive acid can affect flavor.
- **Adjustments:** For low-acid foods, make sure the acid level is set according to tested recipes. To ensure proper preservation of high-acid foods, use the prescribed amount.

The proper use of sugar, salt, and acid is essential for successful canning. These components help to guarantee that the preserved food is safe, flavorful and retains the desired texture and quality.

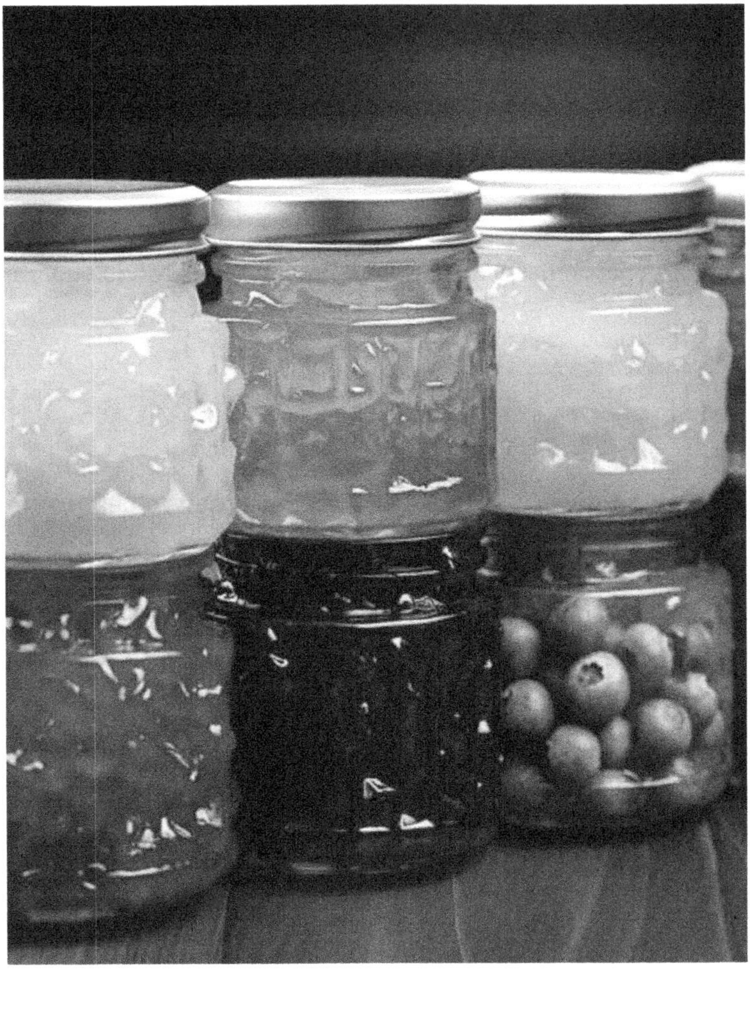

STEP-BY-STEP CANNING PROCESSES

Water Bath Canning

Preparedness

- **Select and Prepare Ingredients:** Choose foods high in acid, such as fruits, juices, jams, jellies, and pickles. Wash, peel, and cut as necessary.
- **sterilize jars and lids:** Wash jars and lids with hot, soapy water. Jars can be sterilized by boiling them for 10 minutes or running them through a hot dishwasher. To soften the sealing compound, simmer the lids in hot water (but not boiling).
- **Prepare the canning pot:** Make sure you have a wide, deep pot with a rack or a canning adapter that can accommodate jars in a single layer. The pot should be tall enough to cover the jars with at least an inch of water.

Fill Jars

- **Prepare food:** Prepare the food according to the instructions in the recipe, including any cooking or pre-processing processes.
- **Fill the Jars:** Fill the prepared food into jars using a canning funnel. Leave the necessary headspace (typically 1/4 to 1/2 inch) as recommended in the recipe.
- **Remove air bubbles:** Using a bubble remover or a clean spatula, gently stir around the jar's edges to liberate trapped air bubbles.
- **Wipe rims:** Wipe the jar rims with a clean, moist cloth to remove any food particles or residue that may hinder a proper seal.
- **Apply lids:** Place the sterilized lid on each jar and screw on the metal band (ring) until it is fingertip tight. Don't over tighten.

Processing: Heat water.

Place the jars in the canning pot, using the rack or canning insert. Add enough hot water to cover the jars by at least an inch.

- **Boil:** Heat the water to a roaring boil. Begin timing the operation when the water comes to a full, rolling boil. Process for the time provided in the recipe.
- **Maintain Boil:** Keep the water at a steady, strong boil throughout the processing time.

Cooling & Storage

- **Remove jars:** After the processing time is up, use jar lifters to carefully remove the jars from the hot water. Place the jars on a clean, dry cloth or cooling rack, leaving enough space between them for air circulation.
- **Cool:** Allow jars to cool completely at room temperature, usually for 12 to 24 hours. To guarantee optimal seal formation, do not touch or move the jars while they cool.

- **Check seals:** After cooling, test the seal by pressing it in the center of each lid. If it's concave and doesn't move, the seal is probably intact. If the lid lifts or moves, the jar is not properly sealed.
- **Label and store:** Label each jar with the contents and the date of processing. Store them somewhere cool, dark, and dry. Depending on the type of food and storage circumstances, properly canned items can survive anywhere from months to years.

Following these instructions allows you to safely and successfully preserve high-acid foods using the water bath canning process. This approach is great for preserving the flavor and freshness of fruits, jams, and pickles.

Pressure Canning

Preparedness

- **Select and Prepare Ingredients:** Choose foods with low acidity, such as veggies, meats, and poultry. Wash, peel, cut, and prepare according to the recipe.

- **sterilize jars and lids:** Wash jars and lids with hot, soapy water. Jars can be sterilized by boiling them for 10 minutes or running them through a hot dishwasher. To soften the sealing compound, simmer **the lids in hot water (but not boiling).**
- **Prepare the pressure canner:** Make sure your pressure canner is clean and in good working order. Inspect the gasket, vent, and pressure gauge. Ensure that the canner is large enough to hold the jars in a single layer and can sustain the proper pressure.

Fill Jars

- **Prepare food:** Cook or pre-process the food according to the directions in the recipe, such as blanching vegetables or pre-cooking meats.
- **Fill the Jars:** Fill the prepared food into jars using a canning funnel. Leave the necessary headroom (typically 1 inch) as mentioned in the recipe.

- **Remove air bubbles:** Using a bubble remover or a clean spatula, gently stir around the jar's edges to liberate trapped air bubbles.
- **Wipe rims:** Wipe the jar rims with a clean, moist cloth to remove any food particles or residue that may hinder a proper seal.
- **Apply lids:** Place the sterilized lid on each jar and screw on the metal band (ring) until it is fingertip tight. Don't over tighten.

Processing.

- **Add water to the canner:** Add the amount of water suggested in the pressure canner's instructions, which is usually 2 to 3 inches, to the bottom of the canner.
- **Load jars:** Place the jars on a canner rack or trivet. Make sure they don't touch each other or the sides of the canner.
- **Seal the canner:** Secure and lock the lid of the canner according to the manufacturer's instructions.

- **Vent steam:** Heat the canner on medium-high until steam begins to escape out the vent. Allow the canner to release steam for 10 minutes to verify all air has been removed.
- **Seal and build pressure:** Close the vent using the weight or adjust the vent valve as directed. Allow the canner to develop pressure. Monitor the pressure gauge until you reach the desired pressure level for your recipe.
- **Process:** Once the canner has reached the appropriate pressure, begin timing. Maintain the pressure for the entire processing time stated in the recipe. Adjust the heat as needed to maintain a constant pressure.

Cooling and Storage:

- **Release Pressure:** Once the processing is complete, turn off the heat and let the canner cool naturally. Do not open the canner until the pressure has been completely released and the gauge shows zero.

- **Remove jars:** Using jar lifters, carefully remove jars from the canner. Place the jars on a clean, dry cloth or cooling rack, leaving enough space between them for air circulation.
- **Cool:** Allow jars to cool completely at room temperature, usually for 12 to 24 hours. To guarantee optimal seal formation, do not touch or move the jars while they cool.
- **Check seals:** After cooling, test the seal by pressing it in the center of each lid. If it's concave and doesn't move, the seal is probably intact. If the lid lifts or moves, the jar is not properly sealed.
- **Label and store:** Label each jar with the contents and the date of processing. Store them somewhere cool, dark, and dry. Depending on the type of food and storage circumstances, properly canned items can survive anywhere from months to years.

Pressure canning is necessary for safely preserving low-acid foods. By following these methods, you can ensure that your preserved foods are safe, tasty, and shelf-stable.

Troubleshooting Common Issues

Jars Not Sealing Properly Problem:

Lids do not create a vacuum seal.

Possible causes:

- **Improper Headspace:** Excessive or insufficient headspace can inhibit proper sealing. Make sure you follow the recipe's headspace requirements.
- **Food Particles on Rims:** Residue or food particles on jar rims might hinder lids from sealing properly. Before attaching lids, wipe the rims with a clean, moist cloth.
- **Damaged Jars or Lids:** Jars that are cracked or chipped, as well as lids with damaged sealing materials, will not seal. Before using jars and lids, inspect them for any damage.
- **Insufficient Processing Time:** Under processing can lead to an unsatisfactory seal. Make sure to follow the precise processing time stated in the recipe.

Solutions:

- **Adjust Headspace:** Remove any extra food or add more as needed, then replace the lid and proceed again if possible.
- **Clean Rims:** Wipe the jar rims completely before sealing.
- **Check for damage:** Use only undamaged jars with fresh lids. Reprocess jars with new lids if necessary.

Cloudy or Off-Color Liquid Problem:

The liquid in jars is cloudy or has changed color.

Possible causes:

Food that has been overcooked or improperly processed may seem cloudy or discolored. Follow the recipe instructions closely.

Excess air bubbles can reduce liquid clarity. Before sealing, make sure to remove all air bubbles.

Improper Acid Levels: Insufficient acid in high-acid foods might produce discoloration. Use the exact amount of acid given in the recipe.

Solutions:

- **Reprocess:** If the cloudiness is caused by overcooking, it may be required to reprocess the meal using suitable protocols.
- **Adjust Acid Levels:** To avoid discoloration, make sure you use the correct amount of acid in the recipe.

Floating Food Problem:

Food rises to the top of the jar during processing.

Possible causes:

- **Over packing:** When jars are over packed, food may float. To ensure good packing, follow the recipe directions.

Inadequate headspace can cause food to float. Ensure that proper headspace is maintained.

Solutions:

- **Repack Jars:** To avoid over packing, adjust the amount of food in each jar. Reprocess if necessary to retain the proper headspace.

Jars fail to seal after processing.

Possible causes:

- **Temperature Fluctuations:** Rapid temperature variations during processing or cooling may prevent sealing. Allow the jars to cool gradually at room temperature.

Insufficient processing time can result in open jars. Ensure that appropriate processing times are followed.

Solutions:

- **Reprocessing:** If jars do not seal, they can be refrigerated and reused within a few days. Alternatively, reprocess with new lids and follow the correct processes.

Soft or Mushy Food Problem:

Food has become soft or mushy after canning.

Possible causes:

Overcooking or excessive processing might result in a mushy texture. Follow the required cooking time and processing instructions.

- **Low-Quality food:** Using overripe or poor-quality food might cause a mushy texture. Choose fresh, high-quality ingredients.

Solutions:

- **Adjust Cooking periods:** Follow the cooking and processing periods stated in the recipe.
- **Use Fresh vegetables:** To preserve the correct texture, use only fresh, high-quality vegetables.

Mold on Food Problem:

Mold forms on the surface of canned foods.

Possible causes:

- **Improper Sealing:** Mold can grow if jars are not properly sealed. Ensure that jars are correctly sealed and processed.

Inadequate processing time might cause mold growth. Follow the recipe's processing time and temperature specifications.

Solutions:

Reprocess any jars that did not seal correctly. If mold appears, toss the jar as it may suggest spoiling.

Understanding these typical concerns and their remedies allows you to efficiently troubleshoot problems and achieve good canning results.

61 | JULIA M. MOODY

RECIPES FOR BEGINNERS

Simple Jams and Jellies

Strawberry Jam

Ingredients.

4 cups fresh strawberries, hulled and mashed.

1/4 cup lemon juice.

5 cups granulated sugar.

1 package (1.75 oz.) fruit pectin (like Sure-Jell)

Instructions:

- **Prepare jars and lids:** Clean and sterilize the jars and lids. Keep them heated until they're ready to use.
- **Prepare Fruit:** Mash strawberries to the desired consistency. Combine with lemon juice in a big pot.
- **Cook Jam:** Stir in the fruit pectin and bring to a boil over medium heat, stirring constantly. Once boiling, add the sugar all at once. Stir thoroughly and bring to a full, rolling boil. Boil for 1-2 minutes, or until the

jam has reached the gel stage (use a thermometer to measure 220°F or a cold plate test).

- **Fill the Jars:** Pour hot jam into hot sterilized jars, leaving 1/4 inch of headspace. To remove any remaining residue, wipe the rims with a clean, wet cloth. Screw on metal bands until fingertip tight.
- **Process:** Boil the jars for 5 minutes. Adjust the time for altitude as needed.
- **Cool and Store:** Allow jars to cool completely on a clean cloth or rack. Check seals, label, and keep them in a cool, dark area.

Blueberry Jelly

Ingredients

4 cups fresh or frozen blueberries.

1/4 cup lemon juice.

1 package (1.75 ounces) fruit pectin (like Sure-Jell)

5 cups granulated sugar.

Instructions:

- **Prepare jars and lids:** Clean and sterilize the jars and lids. Keep them heated until they're ready to use.
- **Prepare Fruit:** In a big pot, crush the blueberries and bring to a boil. Reduce the heat to a simmer for 10 minutes. To extract juice, strain through a fine mesh strainer or cheesecloth.
- **Cook Jelly:** Measure 3. Add 1/2 cup blueberry juice and return to the pot. Stir in the lemon juice and fruit pectin. Bring to a boil over medium heat, stirring continuously. Add the sugar all at once and bring to a rolling boil. Boil for 1–2 minutes, or until the jelly reaches 220°F.
- **Fill the Jars:** Pour heated jelly into hot sterilized jars, leaving 1/4 inch of headspace. Wipe the rims with a clean, moist towel. Screw on metal bands until fingertip tight.
- **Process:** Boil the jars for 5 minutes. Adjust the time for altitude as needed.
- **Cool and Store:** Allow jars to cool completely on a clean cloth or rack. Check seals, label them, and keep them in a cool, dark area.

Apple Jelly

Ingredients

4 cups apple juice, preferably freshly pressed.

1/4 cup lemon juice.

1 package (1.75 oz.) fruit pectin (like Sure-Jell)

5 cups granulated sugar.

Instructions:

- **Prepare jars and lids:** Clean and sterilize the jars and lids. Keep them heated until they're ready to use.
- **Cook Jelly:** In a big pot, mix apple juice, lemon juice, and fruit pectin. Bring to a boil on medium heat, stirring frequently. Add the sugar all at once and bring to a rolling boil. Boil for 1–2 minutes, or until the jelly reaches 220°F.
- **Fill the Jars:** Pour heated jelly into hot sterilized jars, leaving 1/4 inch of headspace. Wipe the rims with a clean, moist towel. Screw on metal bands until fingertip tight.

- **Process:** Boil the jars for 5 minutes. Adjust the time for altitude as needed.
- **Cool and Store:** Allow jars to cool completely on a clean cloth or rack. Check seals, label, and keep in a cool, dark area.

These basic recipes are ideal for novices and provide an excellent start to producing jams and jellies. They are simple, use few ingredients, and produce wonderful homemade preserves.

Pickles and Relishes

Classic Dill Pickles

Ingredients:

6 cups of water.

1/2 cup of white vinegar.

1/4 cup granulated sugar.

1/4 cup pickling salt.

4 garlic cloves, peeled

2 teaspoons dill seeds or 4-6 sprigs of fresh dill

1 teaspoon of black peppercorns.

1/2 teaspoon of red pepper flakes (optional)

4-6 tiny cucumbers (pickling or Kirby variety).

Instructions:

- **Prepare jars and lids:** Clean and sterilize the jars and lids. Keep them heated until they're ready to use.
- **Prepare Brine:** In a large pot, combine the water, vinegar, sugar, and pickling salt. Bring to a boil, stirring until sugar and salt are dissolved. Remove from heat and allow it to cool slightly.
- **Prepare cucumbers:** Wash the cucumbers thoroughly. If using a larger cucumber, cut it into spears or slices.
- **Pack jars:** Put garlic cloves, dill, peppercorns, and red pepper flakes (if using) in each jar. Pack cucumbers securely into jars, leaving about a half-inch headspace.

- **Add brine:** Pour hot brine over cucumbers, covering them fully. Leave a 1/2-inch headspace. Wipe the rims with a clean, moist towel.
- **Sealing and Processing:** Screw on metal bands until fingertip tight. Boil the jars for 10 minutes.
- **Cool and Store:** Allow jars to cool completely on a clean cloth or rack. Check seals, label them, and keep them in a cool, dark area. To achieve the finest flavor, let pickles cure for at least 2-4 weeks before consuming.

Sweet Pickle Relish.

Ingredients:

4 cups of finely chopped cucumbers.

1 cup finely chopped onion

1/2 cup of finely chopped red bell peppers.

1/4 cup pickling salt.

2 cups granulated sugar and 1 1/2 cups white vinegar

1 tablespoon of mustard seeds.

1 teaspoon of celery seeds.

1/2 teaspoon of ground turmeric.

Instructions:

- **Prepare vegetables:** In a large bowl, combine cucumbers, onions, and red bell peppers. Sprinkle with pickling salt and combine thoroughly. Cover and let stand for 2 hours.
- **Drain and rinse:** Drain the vegetables in a colander. Rinse completely with cold water and drain again.
- **Cook relish:** In a large pot, combine the sugar, vinegar, mustard seeds, celery seeds, and turmeric. Bring to a boil over medium heat, stirring until sugar has dissolved. Add the vegetables and cook for 10 minutes.
- **Prepare jars:** Clean and sterilize the jars and lids. Keep them heated until they're ready to use.
- **Fill the Jars:** Pack hot relish into jars, leaving 1/4 inch of headspace. Wipe the rims with a clean, moist towel.

- **Sealing and Processing:** Screw on metal bands until fingertip tight. Boil the jars for 10 minutes.
- **Cool and Store:** Allow jars to cool completely on a clean cloth or rack. Check seals, label them, and keep them in a cool, dark area. Allow relish to sit for at least 2-4 weeks before serving for the finest flavor.

Spicy Pickled Jalapeños.

Ingredients:

1 pound of fresh jalapeño peppers.

2 cups white vinegar.

Ingredients: 2 cups water, 4 cloves of peeled garlic.

Ingredients: 1 tablespoon sugar, 2 teaspoons pickling salt.

1 teaspoon of dried oregano.

1/2 teaspoon crushed red pepper flakes.

Instructions:

- **Prepare jars and lids:** Clean and sterilize the jars and lids. Keep them heated until they're ready to use.
- **Prepare peppers:** Wash and cut jalapeños into rings. Remove the seeds if you prefer less heat.
- **Prepare Brine:** In a big pot, mix vinegar, water, sugar, pickling salt, and oregano. Bring to a boil, stirring until sugar and salt are dissolved.
- **Pack jars:** Place garlic cloves and crushed red pepper flakes in each container. Pack jalapeño slices in jars.
- **Add brine:** Cover jalapeños with spicy brine. Leave a 1/4-inch headspace. Wipe the rims with a clean, moist towel.
- **Sealing and Processing:** Screw on metal bands until fingertip tight. Boil the jars for 10 minutes.
- **Cool and Store:** Allow jars to cool completely on a clean cloth or rack. Check seals, label them, and keep them in a cool, dark area. Allow it to sit for at least two weeks before serving to develop flavor.

These recipes include a variety of pickle and relish options, which are ideal for adding a tangy, crunchy flavor to your dishes. Enjoy playing with these flavors!

Tomato-Based Products
Homemade Tomato Sauce

Ingredients:

10 pounds of ripe tomatoes.

Use 1 tablespoon lemon juice per pint jar (or 2 tablespoons each quart jar).

1 teaspoon of salt each pint jar (optional).

1/2 teaspoon of black pepper per pint jar (optional).

1 teaspoon dried basil or oregano for each pint jar (optional)

Instructions:

- **Prepare tomatoes:** Wash tomatoes and remove the stems. Blanch them in boiling water for 1-2 minutes before transferring them to icy water. Peel and slice tomatoes.

- **Cook sauce:** Cook chopped tomatoes in a big pot on medium heat. Simmer for around 30 minutes to reduce and thicken, stirring occasionally. Puree the sauce using an immersion blender or food processor to achieve a smoother consistency.
- **Add seasonings:** Add optional salt, pepper, and herbs to taste. Cook for an additional five minutes.
- **Prepare jars:** Clean and sterilize the jars and lids. Keep them heated until they're ready to use.
- **Fill the Jars:** Add 1 tablespoon lemon juice in every pint jar and 2 tablespoons per quart jar. Pour heated tomato sauce into jars, leaving a half-inch headspace. Wipe the rims with a clean, moist towel.
- **Sealing and Processing:** Screw on metal bands until fingertip tight. In a boiling water bath, process pint jars for 35 minutes and quart jars for 45 minutes.
- **Cool and Store:** Allow jars to cool completely on a clean cloth or rack. Check seals, label them, and keep them in a cool, dark area. For optimal flavor, use the sauce within a year.

Tomato Salsa

Ingredients

8 cups chopped tomatoes.

1 cup chopped onions.

1/2 cup of chopped green bell peppers.

1/2 cup chopped red bell peppers.

1/4 cup lime juice.

1 tablespoon chopped fresh cilantro (or one teaspoon dried)

2 garlic cloves, minced

1 teaspoon ground cumin.

1/2 teaspoon of salt.

1/4 teaspoon of black pepper.

1-2 jalapeños, seeded and minced (to taste)

Instructions:

- **Prepare Ingredients:** Wash and cut the vegetables. Mix tomatoes, onions, bell peppers, jalapeños, and garlic in a large bowl.
- **Cook Salsa:** In a large pot, combine the tomatoes, lime juice, cilantro, cumin, salt, and pepper. Bring to a boil on medium heat, stirring frequently. Reduce the heat and let the salsa simmer for 10-15 minutes until it thickens.
- **Prepare jars:** Clean and sterilize the jars and lids. Keep them heated until they're ready to use.
- **Fill the Jars:** Pour heated salsa into jars, leaving a half-inch headspace. Wipe the rims with a clean, moist towel.
- **Sealing and Processing:** Screw on metal bands until fingertip tight. Boil the jars for 15 minutes.
- **Cool and Store:** Allow jars to cool completely on a clean cloth or rack. Check seals, label them, and keep them in a cool, dark area. Salsa should be used within a year for maximum flavor.

Tomato paste

Ingredients:

12 pounds of ripe tomatoes.

Use 1 tablespoon lemon juice per pint jar (or 2 tablespoons each quart jar).

1/2 teaspoon of salt per pint jar (optional).

Instructions:

- **Prepare tomatoes:** Wash tomatoes and remove the stems. Cut into fourths.
- **Cook tomatoes:** Cook tomatoes in a big pot over medium heat until they break down and soften for about 30 minutes. Using a food mill or sieve, remove the peels and seeds, leaving only the tomato pulp.
- **Reduce pulp:** Return the tomato pulp to the pot and cook over low heat, stirring regularly, until it has reduced to a thick paste. This can take anything from one to two hours.
- **Prepare jars:** Clean and sterilize the jars and lids. Keep them heated until they're ready to use.

- **Fill the Jars:** For a pint jar, add 1 tablespoon of lemon juice, and for a quart jar, 2 tablespoons. Pour heated tomato paste into jars, leaving a half-inch headspace. Wipe the rims with a clean, moist towel.
- **Sealing and Processing:** Screw on metal bands until fingertip tight. In a boiling water bath, process pint jars for 35 minutes and quart jars for 45 minutes.
- Cool and Store: Allow jars to cool completely on a clean cloth or rack. Check seals, label, and keep them in a cool, dark area. Tomato paste should be used within a year for optimal quality.

These tomato-based recipes are ideal for maintaining the fresh flavor of tomatoes. They may be used in a variety of recipes and are excellent additions to your home pantry.

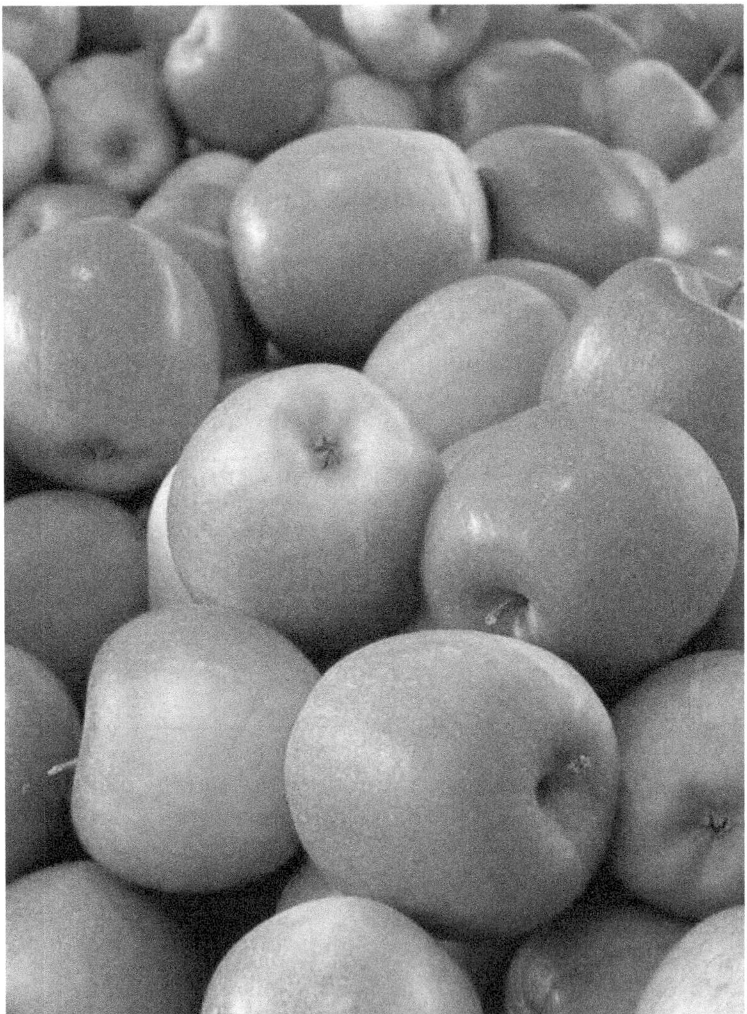

ADVANCED CANNING RECIPES

Preserving Meats and Poultry

Canning Beef Stew

Ingredients:

3 pounds of beef stew meat, chopped into 1-inch pieces.

Add 1 cup chopped onions and 1 cup diced carrots.

1 cup diced potatoes

Ingredients: 1 cup beef broth, 2 cloves minced garlic.

1 teaspoon dried thyme.

1 teaspoon dried rosemary.

1 teaspoon salt.

1/2 teaspoon of black pepper.

One tablespoon of lemon juice per quart jar.

Instructions:

- **Prepare jars and lids:** Clean and sterilize the jars and lids. Keep them heated until they're ready to use.
- **Brown Meat:** In a large skillet, brown the meat cubes in batches over medium-high heat. Transfer to a big bowl.
- **Prepare vegetables:** In the same skillet, cook the onions and garlic until tender. Add the carrots and potatoes and simmer for a few minutes.
- **Pack jars:** Pour 1 tablespoon of lemon juice into each quart jar. Pack meat, veggies, and any remaining liquid into jars, leaving 1 inch of headspace.
- **Add broth and seasonings:** Pour beef broth over the contents of each jar, allowing 1 inch of headspace. Add salt, pepper, thyme, and rosemary.
- **Sealing and Processing:** Wipe the rims with a clean, moist towel. Screw on metal bands until fingertip tight. Process jars in a pressure canner at 10-15 pounds of pressure for 75 minutes for pints and 90 minutes for quarts.

- **Cool and Store:** Allow jars to cool completely on a clean cloth or rack. Check seals, label them, and keep them in a cool, dark area.

Canning Chicken

Ingredients

4 pounds of boneless, skinless chicken breasts or thighs, chopped into bits.

1/2 cup of chicken broth per jar (optional)

One teaspoon of salt per pint jar.

1/2 teaspoon of black pepper per pint jar.

Use 1/2 teaspoon dried thyme per pint jar (optional).

One tablespoon of lemon juice per pint jar.

Instructions:

- **Prepare jars and lids:** Clean and sterilize the jars and lids. Keep them heated until they're ready to use.

- **Pack jars:** Pour 1 tablespoon of lemon juice into each pint jar. Pack chicken pieces into jars, leaving 1 inch of headspace. Add salt, pepper, and thyme to each jar.
- **Add Broth (optional):** If preferred, add 1/2 cup of chicken broth to each jar.
- **Sealing and Processing:** Wipe the rims with a clean, moist towel. Screw on metal bands until fingertip tight. Process jars in a pressure canner at 10-15 pounds of pressure for 75 minutes for pints and 90 minutes for quarts.
- **Cool and Store:** Allow jars to cool completely on a clean cloth or rack. Check seals, label them, and keep them in a cool, dark area.

Canning Pork Tenderloin

Ingredients:

4 pounds of pork tenderloin, sliced into 1-inch cubes.

1/2 cup of apple cider vinegar.

Combine 1/2 cup water, 2 teaspoons salt, and 1 teaspoon black pepper.

1 teaspoon of dried sage.

1 teaspoon dried rosemary.

One tablespoon of lemon juice per pint jar.

Instructions:

- **Prepare jars and lids:** Clean and sterilize the jars and lids. Keep them heated until they're ready to use.
- **Prepare meat:** In a large skillet, brown the pork cubes in batches over medium-high heat. Transfer to a big bowl.
- **Pack jars:** Pour 1 tablespoon of lemon juice into each pint jar. Pack pork cubes into jars, leaving 1 inch of headspace.
- **Add vinegar and seasonings:** In a separate bowl, mix apple cider vinegar, water, salt, pepper, sage, and rosemary. Pour mixture over pork chunks in jars, leaving 1 inch of headspace.

- **Sealing and Processing:** Wipe the rims with a clean, moist towel. Screw on metal bands until fingertip tight. Process jars in a pressure canner at 10-15 pounds of pressure for 75 minutes for pints and 90 minutes for quarts.
- **Cool and Store:** Allow jars to cool completely on a clean cloth or rack. Check seals, label them, and keep them in a cool, dark area.

Canned chicken broth:

Ingredients

4-5 pounds of chicken carcass or bones.

Chop 1 onion, 2 carrots, and 2 celery stalks. Mince 2 garlic cloves. Add 1 bay leaf and 1 teaspoon of dry thyme.

Add salt and pepper to taste.

Water

Instructions:

- **Prepare the broth:** Place the chicken carcass, onions, carrots, celery, garlic, bay leaf, and thyme in a large stockpot. Pour enough water to cover the ingredients. Bring to a boil, then reduce the heat and simmer for 2-3 hours.
- **Strain broth:** Strain the broth into another saucepan using a fine-mesh strainer or cheesecloth, discarding any particles.
- **Prepare jars and lids:** Clean and sterilize the jars and lids. Keep them heated until they're ready to use.
- **Fill the Jars:** Pour heated broth into hot jars, leaving 1 inch of headspace.
- **Sealing and Processing:** Wipe the rims with a clean, moist towel. Screw on metal bands until fingertip tight. Process jars in a pressure canner at 10-15 pounds of pressure for 20 minutes for pints and 25 minutes for quarts.
- **Cool and Store:** Allow jars to cool completely on a clean cloth or rack. Check seals, label, and keep in a cool, dark area.

These advanced meat and poultry canning recipes offer flavorful and convenient solutions for preserving meals at home. Follow correct canning processes and adjust processing periods based on altitude to ensure safe preservation.

Canning Soups and Stews

Beef and Vegetable Stew

Ingredients:

2 pounds of beef stew meat, chopped into 1-inch pieces.

Two cups of chopped onions and carrots.

2 cups chopped potatoes

Ingredients: 1 cup chopped celery, 1 cup diced tomatoes.

4 garlic cloves, minced

Ingredients: 1 cup beef broth, 1 teaspoon dried thyme, 1 teaspoon dry rosemary.

1 teaspoon salt.

1/2 teaspoon of black pepper.

1 tablespoon lemon juice per quart jar.

Instructions:

- **Prepare jars and lids:** Clean and sterilize the jars and lids. Keep them heated until they're ready to use.
- **Brown Meat:** Cook beef chunks in a large skillet over medium-high heat. Transfer to a big bowl.
- **Prepare vegetables:** In the same skillet, cook the onions, garlic, carrots, potatoes, celery, and tomatoes until softened.
- **Pack jars:** Pour 1 tablespoon of lemon juice into each quart jar. Pack beef and veggies into jars, leaving 1 inch of headspace.
- **Add broth and seasonings:** Pour the beef broth over the contents of each jar. Combine thyme, rosemary, salt, and pepper.
- **Sealing and Processing:** Wipe the rims with a clean, moist towel. Screw on metal bands until fingertip tight. For quart jars, process them in a pressure canner at 10-15 pounds of pressure for 75 minutes.

- **Cool and Store:** Allow jars to cool completely on a clean cloth or rack. Check seals, label, and keep them in a cool, dark area.

Chicken and Rice Soup

Ingredients:

2 pounds of boneless, skinless chicken breasts or thighs, chopped into bits.

2 cups chopped onions, 1 cup chopped celery, and 1 cup chopped carrots

1 cup of cooked rice.

4 garlic cloves, minced

Ingredients: 1 cup chicken broth, 1 teaspoon dried basil.

Ingredients: 1 teaspoon dried parsley, 1 teaspoon salt.

1/2 teaspoon of black pepper.

1 tablespoon lemon juice per quart jar.

Instructions:

- **Prepare jars and lids:** Clean and sterilize the jars and lids. Keep them heated until they're ready to use.
- **Cook chicken:** In a large skillet, sauté chicken chunks until they are no longer pink. Transfer to a big bowl.
- **Prepare vegetables:** In the same skillet, sauté the onions, celery, carrots, and garlic until tender.
- **Pack jars:** Pour 1 tablespoon of lemon juice into each quart jar. Pack chicken, vegetables, and cooked rice into jars, leaving 1 inch of headspace.
- **Add broth and seasonings:** Pour chicken broth over the contents of each jar. Combine basil, parsley, salt, and pepper.
- **Sealing and Processing:** Wipe the rims with a clean, moist towel. Screw on metal bands until fingertip tight. For quart jars, process them in a pressure canner at 10-15 pounds of pressure for 75 minutes.
- **Cool and Store:** Allow jars to cool completely on a clean cloth or rack. Check seals, label them, and keep them in a cool, dark area.

Tomato-based Minestrone Soup

Ingredients:

4 cups chopped tomatoes.

Ingredients: 1 cup chopped onions, carrots, celery, green beans.

1 cup of diced zucchini.

1 cup cooked pasta.

4 garlic cloves, minced

1 teaspoon of dried oregano.

1 teaspoon dried basil.

1 teaspoon salt and 1/2 teaspoon black pepper.

1 tablespoon lemon juice per quart jar.

Instructions:

- Prepare jars and lids: Clean and sterilize the jars and lids. Keep them heated until they're ready to use.

- **Prepare vegetables:** In a large pot, sauté the onions, garlic, carrots, celery, and green beans until tender.
- **Add tomatoes and seasonings:** Add the diced tomatoes, zucchini, oregano, basil, salt and pepper. Simmer for ten minutes.
- **Pack jars:** Pour 1 tablespoon of lemon juice into each quart jar. Pack the soup mixture into jars, leaving 1 inch of headspace. Add the cooked spaghetti.
- **Sealing and Processing:** Wipe the rims with a clean, moist towel. Screw on metal bands until fingertip tight. For quart jars, process them in a pressure canner at 10-15 pounds of pressure for 75 minutes.
- **Cool and Store:** Allow jars to cool completely on a clean cloth or rack. Check seals, label them, and keep them in a cool, dark area.

These advanced soup and stew recipes are ideal for canning enthusiasts looking to preserve hearty, flavorful meals. Proper processing and storage ensure that soups and stews retain their flavor and quality.

Complex Sauces and Condiments
Homemade Barbecue Sauce

Ingredients

2 cups ketchup.

1 cup apple cider vinegar.

1/2 cup brown sugar.

1/2 cup honey and 1/4 cup soy sauce.

2 tablespoons Worcestershire sauce.

2 teaspoons of lemon juice.

2 garlic cloves, minced

1 teaspoon of smoked paprika.

1/2 teaspoon of black pepper.

1/2 teaspoon of ground cumin

1/2 teaspoon of chili powder.

Instructions:

- **Combine Ingredients:** In a large saucepan, combine the ketchup, apple cider vinegar, brown sugar, honey, soy sauce, Worcestershire sauce, and lemon juice. Stir in the garlic, smoked paprika, black pepper, cumin, and chili powder.
- **Cook sauce:** Bring to a boil on medium heat, stirring frequently. Reduce heat to a simmer for 20-30 minutes, or until the sauce thickens and the flavors blend. Stir occasionally.
- **Prepare jars and lids:** Clean and sterilize the jars and lids. Keep them heated until they're ready to use.
- **Fill the Jars:** Pour hot barbecue sauce into jars, leaving 1/4 inch of headspace. Wipe the rims with a clean, moist towel.
- **Sealing and Processing:** Screw on metal bands until fingertip tight. Boil the jars for 15 minutes.
- **Cool and Store:** Allow jars to cool completely on a clean cloth or rack. Check seals, label them, and keep them in a cool, dark area. For optimal flavor, use the sauce within a year.

Spicy Salsa Verde.

Ingredients:

2 pounds of tomatillos, husked and chopped

1 cup chopped onions and 1/2 cup chopped cilantro.

Ingredients: 2 minced garlic cloves, 1-2 seeded and minced jalapeños (to taste).

1/2 cup of lime juice.

1 teaspoon salt and 1/2 teaspoon black pepper.

Instructions:

- **Prepare Ingredients:** In a large pot, mix tomatillos, onions, cilantro, garlic, and jalapeños. Bring to a boil, then reduce the heat and simmer for 10-15 minutes, or until the tomatillos are tender.
- **Blend salsa:** Blend the salsa until smooth using an immersion blender or a food processor. Return to the pot and cook for an additional 10 minutes until thickened.

- **Prepare jars and lids:** Clean and sterilize the jars and lids. Keep them heated until they're ready to use.
- **Fill the Jars:** Pour 1 tablespoon lime juice and 1/2 teaspoon salt into each pint jar. Pour hot salsa verde into jars, leaving a half-inch headspace. Wipe the rims with a clean, moist towel.
- **Sealing and Processing:** Screw on metal bands until fingertip tight. Boil the jars for 15 minutes.
- **Cool and Store:** Allow jars to cool completely on a clean cloth or rack. Check seals, label them, and keep them in a cool, dark area. Salsa Verde tastes best when used within a year.

Gourmet Mustard

Ingredients:

1 cup yellow mustard seeds.

1/2 cup of brown mustard seeds.

1 cup of white wine vinegar.

1/2 cup water, 1/4 cup honey, 1 tablespoon sugar, 1 teaspoon salt, and 1/2 teaspoon ground turmeric.

1/2 teaspoon of ground paprika.

Instructions:

- **Soak mustard seeds:** In a bowl, blend yellow and brown mustard seeds, vinegar, and water. Cover and allow it to soak for 24 hours.
- **Blend mustard:** Transfer the mustard seeds and liquid to a blender or food processor. Combine honey, sugar, salt, turmeric, and paprika. Blend until your desired consistency is obtained.
- **Prepare jars and lids:** Clean and sterilize the jars and lids. Keep them heated until they're ready to use.
- **Fill the Jars:** Pour mustard into jars, leaving 1/4 inch of headspace. Wipe the rims with a clean, moist towel.
- **Sealing and Processing:** Screw on metal bands until fingertip tight. Boil the jars for 10 minutes.
- **Cool and Store:** Allow jars to cool completely on a clean cloth or rack. Check seals, label them, and keep them in a cool, dark area. Mustard tastes best when consumed within a year.

Pickled hot peppers.

Ingredients:

1 pound sliced jalapeños or serrano's, and 2 cups white vinegar.

1 cup water.

Ingredients: 1/4 cup sugar, 2 cloves of chopped garlic, and 1 tablespoon salt.

1 teaspoon of dried oregano.

1/2 teaspoon of black peppercorns.

1/2 teaspoon of mustard seeds.

Instructions:

- **Prepare jars and lids:** Clean and sterilize the jars and lids. Keep them heated until they're ready to use.
- **Prepare Brine:** In a big pot, mix vinegar, water, sugar, and salt. Bring to a boil, stirring until sugar and salt are dissolved.

- **Pack jars:** Place garlic, oregano, black peppercorns, and mustard seeds in each container. Pack the cut peppers into jars.
- **Add brine:** Pour hot brine over peppers, leaving 1/4 inch of headspace. Wipe the rims with a clean, moist towel.
- **Sealing and Processing:** Screw on metal bands until fingertip tight. Boil the jars for 10 minutes.
- **Cool and Store:** Allow jars to cool completely on a clean cloth or rack. Check seals, label them, and keep them in a cool, dark area. Allow peppers to pickle for at least 2-3 weeks before eating for the finest flavor.

These complex sauces and condiments provide depth and flavor to a variety of recipes, and with proper canning processes, they may be enjoyed all year round.

SEASONAL AND REGIONAL RECIPES
Canning with Seasonal Produce
Spring Asparagus Spears

Ingredients:

2 pounds of fresh asparagus spears.

1 cup white vinegar.

Ingredients: 1 cup water, 1 tablespoon salt, 1 tablespoon sugar, and 2 cloves of peeled garlic.

1 teaspoon dried dill or 2 sprigs of fresh dill

1/2 teaspoon of black peppercorns.

Instructions:

- **Prepare jars and lids:** Clean and sterilize the jars and lids. Keep them heated until they're ready to use.
- **Prepare asparagus:** Trim the rough ends of asparagus spears. Boil for 2 minutes, then transfer to ice water to cool.

- **Prepare Brine:** In a saucepan, mix vinegar, water, salt, and sugar. Bring to a boil, stirring until the salt and sugar are dissolved.
- **Pack jars:** Put garlic, dill, and peppercorns in each jar. Pack asparagus spears tightly into jars.
- **Add brine:** Pour hot brine over asparagus, allowing a half-inch headspace. Wipe the rims with a clean, moist towel.
- **Sealing and Processing:** Screw on metal bands until fingertip tight. Boil the jars for 10 minutes.
- **Cool and Store:** Allow jars to cool completely on a clean cloth or rack. Check seals, label them, and keep them in a cool, dark area. For the finest flavor, allow to pickle for at least two weeks before consumption.

Summer Tomato Sauce

Ingredients:

10 pounds of ripe tomatoes.

1 cup chopped onions.

4 garlic cloves, minced

1/4 cup olive oil.

1 teaspoon dried basil.

1 teaspoon of dried oregano.

One tablespoon of lemon juice per pint jar.

Salt to taste (optional).

Instructions:

- **Prepare jars and lids:** Clean and sterilize the jars and lids. Keep them heated until they're ready to use.
- **Prepare tomatoes:** Wash the tomatoes and cut them into quarters. Blanch in boiling water for 1-2 minutes before transferring to icy water. Peel and slice tomatoes.
- **Cook sauce:** In a large pot, heat the olive oil over medium heat. Sauté the onions and garlic until softened. Combine tomatoes, basil, and oregano. Simmer for approximately one hour, stirring regularly, until the sauce thickens.

- **Blend Sauce:** To achieve a smoother texture, mix the sauce in an immersion blender or food processor until smooth.
- **Fill the Jars:** Add 1 tablespoon lemon juice to each pint jar. Pour heated tomato sauce into jars, leaving a half-inch headspace. Wipe the rims with a clean, moist towel.
- **Sealing and Processing:** Screw on metal bands until fingertip tight. In a boiling water bath, process pint jars for 35 minutes and quart jars for 45 minutes.
- **Cool and Store:** Allow jars to cool completely on a clean cloth or rack. Check seals, label them, and keep them in a cool, dark area.

Fall Pumpkin Butter

Ingredients

4 cups canned or pureed pumpkin.

1 cup apple cider.

1 cup packed brown sugar.

1 teaspoon ground cinnamon.

1/2 teaspoon of ground nutmeg.

1/4 teaspoon ground cloves.

1/4 teaspoon of ground ginger.

1/4 cup of lemon juice per pint jar.

Instructions:

- **Prepare jars and lids:** Clean and sterilize the jars and lids. Keep them heated until they're ready to use.
- **Cook Pumpkin Butter:** In a large pot, combine the pumpkin, apple cider, brown sugar, and spices. Cook for 30-40 minutes over medium heat, stirring constantly, until thickened and smooth.
- **Fill the Jars:** Add 1/4 cup lemon juice to each pint jar. Pour hot pumpkin butter into jars, leaving 1/4 inch of headspace. Wipe the rims with a clean, moist towel.
- **Sealing and Processing:** Screw on metal bands until fingertip tight. Boil the jars for 10 minutes.
- **Cool and Store:** Allow jars to cool completely on a clean cloth or rack. Check seals, label them, and keep

them in a cool, dark area. Pumpkin butter tastes best when used within a year.

Winter Root Vegetable Pickle

Ingredients:

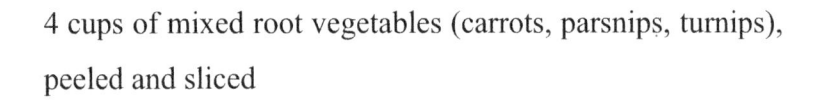

4 cups of mixed root vegetables (carrots, parsnips, turnips), peeled and sliced

2 cups white vinegar.

1 cup water.

1/4 cup sugar.

2 teaspoons of salt.

2 garlic cloves, peeled

1 tablespoon of mustard seeds.

1 tablespoon of coriander seeds.

1 teaspoon dried thyme.

Instructions:

- **Prepare jars and lids:** Clean and sterilize the jars and lids. Keep them heated until they're ready to use.
- **Prepare vegetables:** Boil root veggies in water for 2-3 minutes. To cool, transfer to ice water.
- **Prepare Brine:** In a saucepan, mix vinegar, water, sugar, and salt. Bring to a boil, stirring until sugar and salt are dissolved.
- **Pack jars:** Put garlic, mustard seeds, coriander seeds, and thyme in each container. Pack the vegetables tightly into jars.
- **Add brine:** Pour hot brine over vegetables, allowing a half-inch headspace. Wipe the rims with a clean, moist towel.
- **Sealing and Processing:** Screw on metal bands until fingertip tight. Boil the jars for 15 minutes.
- **Cool and Store:** Allow jars to cool completely on a clean cloth or rack. Check seals, label them, and keep them in a cool, dark area. For the finest flavor, allow to pickle for at least two weeks before consumption.

These seasonal and regional dishes take advantage of fresh, local produce throughout the year, providing a range of flavors and textures to enjoy all year.

Regional Specialties Across the United States

Southern Pickled Okra

Ingredients:

1 pound of fresh okra pods.

1 cup white vinegar.

1 cup water.

1/4 cup pickling salt.

2 garlic cloves, peeled

1 teaspoon of dill seeds.

1/2 teaspoon of red pepper flakes (optional)

Instructions:

- **Prepare jars and lids:** Clean and sterilize the jars and lids. Keep them heated until they're ready to use.
- **Prepare Okra:** Wash okra pods and trim stems. Boil for 2 minutes, then transfer to ice water to cool.
- **Prepare Brine:** In a saucepan, mix vinegar, water, and pickling salt. Bring to a boil and whisk until the salt dissolves.
- **Pack jars:** Put garlic, dill seeds, and optional red pepper flakes in each jar. Pack the okra pods tightly into jars.
- **Add brine:** Pour hot brine over okra, allowing a half-inch headspace. Wipe the rims with a clean, moist towel.
- **Sealing and Processing:** Screw on metal bands until fingertip tight. Boil the jars for 15 minutes.
- **Cool and Store:** Allow jars to cool completely on a clean cloth or rack. Check seals, label, and keep them in a cool, dark area. Pickled okra is finest after about 2-3 weeks of curing.

New England Baked Beans.

Ingredients:

1 pound of dried navy beans.

1/2-pound salt pork sliced into chunks.

1 cup molasses.

1/2 cup brown sugar.

1/2 cup diced onion

2 tablespoons Dijon mustard.

1 teaspoon salt.

1/2 teaspoon of black pepper.

Instructions:

- **Prepare beans:** Soak the beans overnight in plenty of water. Drain and rinse.
- **Cook beans:** Bring beans to a boil in a big pot filled with fresh water. Simmer for 1 hour, until the beans are soft. Drain.

- **Prepare Sauce:** In a separate bowl, mix the molasses, brown sugar, onion, mustard, salt, and pepper.
- **Pack jars:** Layer the beans and salt pork in jars. Pour sauce over beans, allowing 1 inch of headroom. Wipe the rims with a clean, moist towel.
- **Sealing and Processing:** Screw on metal bands until fingertip tight. Pint jars should be processed in a boiling water bath for 90 minutes.
- **Cool and Store:** Allow jars to cool completely on a clean cloth or rack. Check seals, label them, and keep them in a cool, dark area. Beans get a richer flavor after a few weeks.

Midwestern Sweet Corn Relish

Ingredients:

4 cups fresh maize kernels (about eight ears)

1 cup of chopped green bell peppers.

1 cup of chopped red bell peppers.

1 cup chopped onions.

1 cup white vinegar.

1 cup granulated sugar.

1/4 cup pickling salt.

1 teaspoon of mustard seeds.

1 teaspoon of celery seeds.

Instructions:

- **Prepare jars and lids:** Clean and sterilize the jars and lids. Keep them heated until they're ready to use.
- **Prepare vegetables:** In a large pot, add the corn, bell peppers, and onion.
- **Prepare Brine:** In a saucepan, mix vinegar, sugar, and pickling salt. Bring to a boil, stirring until sugar and salt are dissolved.
- **Pack jars:** Add mustard and celery seeds to each jar. Pack the veggie mixture into jars.
- **Add brine:** Pour hot brine over vegetables, allowing a half-inch headspace. Wipe the rims with a clean, moist towel.

- **Sealing and Processing:** Screw on metal bands until fingertip tight. Boil the jars for 15 minutes.
- **Cool and Store:** Allow jars to cool completely on a clean cloth or rack. Check seals, label them, and keep them in a cool, dark area. Relish is best after a few weeks to allow the flavors to mingle.

Southwest Salsa

Ingredients:

6 cups diced tomatoes

1 cup chopped onions.

Ingredients: 1 cup chopped green bell pepper, 1 cup chopped red bell pepper.

Add 1/2 cup chopped jalapeños (seeds removed for reduced heat).

1/2 cup of lime juice.

1/4 cup chopped cilantro.

1 teaspoon cumin.

1 teaspoon salt and 1/2 teaspoon black pepper.

Instructions:

- **Prepare jars and lids:** Clean and sterilize the jars and lids. Keep them heated until they're ready to use.
- **Prepare Salsa:** In a big pot, mix tomatoes, onions, bell peppers, jalapeños, lime juice, cilantro, cumin, salt, and pepper. Bring to a boil, then simmer for 10-15 minutes, or until thickened.
- **Fill the Jars:** Pour heated salsa into jars, leaving a half-inch headspace. Wipe the rims with a clean, moist towel.
- **Sealing and Processing:** Screw on metal bands until fingertip tight. Boil the jars for 15 minutes.
- **Cool and Store:** Allow jars to cool completely on a clean cloth or rack. Check seals, label, and keep them in a cool, dark area. Salsa is best savored after a few weeks of allowing the flavors to develop.

These regional specialties highlight the different flavors and customs of the United States, bringing local favorites into your home pantry through the joys of canning.

113 | JULIA M. MOODY

STORAGE AND SHELF LIFE

Proper Storage Conditions

Temperature

- **Optimal Range:** Keep canned foods in a cool, dark environment with a temperature between 50°F to 70°F. Extreme temperatures, both hot and cold, can have an impact on food quality and safety.
- **Avoid Heat Sources:** Keep cans away from heat-producing appliances such as stoves and ovens. High heat might ruin the food or damage the can's seal.

Humidity

Maintain a dry storage environment to avoid rust on can lids and jars. Excess moisture can promote mold growth and food spoilage.

- **Ventilation:** To reduce humidity, ensure that the storage location has appropriate ventilation. Avoid placing cans directly on the floor, particularly in basements or damp places.

Light.

Cans should be stored in the dark to avoid light exposure. Light can impair the quality of many meals, altering their flavor and nutritional value.

- **Avoid Sunlight:** Direct sunlight might cause the can's contents to spoil faster and compromise the can's integrity.

Shelf Organization

- **Maintain cleanliness:** To avoid dust, grime, and vermin, clean the storage room regularly. Ensure that cans are clean of any spills or residue that may attract pests.
- **First in, first out (FIFO):** Use older cans first to guarantee that food is consumed before it has expired. Rotate the stock such that the most current cans are at the back and the older cans are at the front.

Handling

Before storing, inspect cans and jars for signs of deterioration, such as dents, bulges, or rust. Damaged cans should be discarded since they may not be safe to consume.

- **Avoid Over packing:** Don't overfill the storage area. Allow ample room for air movement around the cans and jars to avoid any potential problems.

By adhering to these storage standards, you may extend the shelf life of your canned goods while keeping them safe and high-quality for longer.

Understanding Shelf Life

Shelf life is the amount of time that canned food is safe to eat and in good condition. It depends on the food's stability and the success of the canning procedure.

Factors affecting shelf life

Food shelf life varies depending on the type of food. For example, acidic foods like tomatoes and fruits have shorter shelf life than low-acid items like meats and vegetables.

- **Canning Process:** Proper canning processes, including the optimum processing periods and temperatures, have a substantial impact on shelf life. Inadequate processing might result in rotting or contamination.

Temperature, humidity, and exposure to light all affect shelf life. Storing cans in appropriate conditions helps to keep food fresher for longer.

Signs of Spoilage

Bulging lids suggest probable bacterial development or deterioration. Do not eat if the lid is bulging.

- **Unpleasant Odors:** If the food smells off or rancid, it may be spoilt.
- **Discoloration:** Significant color changes can indicate rotting, however, mild discoloration is natural for certain foods.

Rusty or leaking cans are unsafe and should be discarded. Rust can compromise the seal, resulting in spoiling.

Texture Changes: Unusual textures, such as mushiness or separation of constituents, may indicate spoiling.

Best Practices for Shelf Life

- **Labeling:** Mark cans with the date of canning. This allows you to keep track of the food's age and use older cans first.
- **Rotation:** Use the "first in, first out" strategy to use older canned products before newer ones, which reduces waste.

Regularly examine storage cans for deterioration or damage. Any compromised cans should be removed and discarded immediately.

Expiration dates.

Many commercial canned foods have a use-by date, which serves as a guideline for ensuring optimal quality. These dates are not rigorous safety deadlines but rather reflect when the product is projected to perform at its peak.

Canned products are frequently safe to eat after their expiration date, as long as there are no signs of deterioration. However, quality may degrade over time.

Long-term storage

- **Extended Shelf Life:** Foods that are properly preserved and kept can last for several years, but quality is optimum when consumed within one or two years.
- **Rotation and Consumption:** To maintain freshness and reduce waste, rotate stored things regularly and consume older commodities.

Understanding and monitoring shelf life helps preserve the safety and quality of canned foods, allowing you to eat nutritious and pleasurable meals for months or even years.

Signs of Spoilage

Bulging or swollen lids.

- **Description:** The can's lid appears bulged outward or bloated.

- **Cause:** This could indicate bacterial growth, gas production, or fermentation inside the can. It suggests that there is a possibility of spoiling.
- **Action:** Do not eat the food. Discard the can right away.

Unpleasant Odor

When the container is opened, it emits an unpleasant or putrid odor.

- **Cause:** This typically implies that the food has spoilt, possibly as a result of bacterial contamination or chemical changes.
- **Action:** Avoid eating the meal. Dispose of the can safely.

Discoloration

- **Description:** Significant color changes in the food inside the can, such as darkening or odd hues.

Causes of discoloration include oxidation and rotting. Some color changes are normal, but severe changes may signal a problem.

- **Action:** If paired with additional spoilage indicators, do not ingest the food.

Leaks or rust.

- **Description:** The can is rusted or has evident leaks.
- **Cause:** Rust or leaks can damage the can's seal, resulting in contamination and deterioration.
- **Action:** Avoid consuming food from corroded or leaking cans. Discard them right away.

Texture changes

The food within the can appears mushy, slimy, or of a strange texture.

- **Cause:** Texture changes can indicate deterioration owing to bacterial activity or enzymatic breakdown.
- **Action:** If the texture is odd and is accompanied by additional rotting indicators, avoid eating the food.

Off-Taste

The meal tastes weird, sour, or has an unpleasant flavor.

Causes of taste alterations include rotting and chemical reactions. Even if the food appears to be fine, an odd flavor is a clear indication of rotting.

- **Action:** Do not consume the food. Discard it.

Gas Emissions

When opened, the can emits an exceptional amount of gas or hissing sound.

Cause: Gas emissions may suggest fermentation or bacterial growth within the can.

- **Action:** Avoid eating the meal. Dispose of the can properly.

Mold/Foam

When food is opened, there may be visible mold or foam on the surface.

- **Cause:** Mold or froth can indicate spoilage owing to yeast or bacterial infestation.
- **Action:** Do not eat the food. Discard the can.

Regularly checking for these indicators of spoilage helps to ensure the safety and quality of your canned goods. When in doubt, err on the side of caution and avoid consuming any food that appears to be spoilt.

CREATIVE USES FOR PRESERVED FOODS

Recipes Incorporating Canned Goods

Canned Tomato Basil Soup.

Ingredients:

2 cans (15 oz.) of canned chopped tomatoes

1 can (15 ounces) of tomato sauce

Ingredients: 1 cup chicken or veggie broth, and 1 cup heavy cream.

1 tablespoon of olive oil.

One medium onion, chopped.

3 garlic cloves, minced

1 teaspoon dried basil.

Add salt and pepper to taste.

Fresh basil leaves for garnish (optional).

Instructions:

- **Sauté Aromatics:** In a large pot, heat the olive oil over medium heat. Cook onions and garlic until softened and transparent.
- **Combine Ingredients:** Add the canned chopped tomatoes, tomato sauce, and broth to the pot. Stir in the dried basil, salt, and pepper.
- **Simmer:** Bring the mixture to a boil, then reduce the heat and simmer for 20 minutes.
- **Blend:** Using an immersion blender, mix the soup until smooth. Alternatively, carefully transfer the soup in batches to a blender.
- **Add cream:** Stir in the heavy cream and heat thoroughly. Adjust the seasoning as needed.
- **Serve:** Garnish with fresh basil leaves if preferred. Serve hot, with crusty bread.

Canned Green Bean Casserole.

Ingredients:

2 cans of canned green beans (14.5 oz each), drained

1 can (10.5 ounces) Cream of mushroom soup.

1/2 cup milk.

1 cup French-fried onions

1/2 cup shredded cheddar cheese (optional)

Add salt and pepper to taste.

Instructions:

- **Preheat the Oven:** Preheat the oven to 350°F (175° C).
- **Mix the ingredients:** In a large mixing bowl, combine the green beans, cream of mushroom soup, milk, and half of the French-fried onions. Season with salt and pepper.

- **Transfer to the baking dish:** Transfer the mixture to a greased baking dish. If using, sprinkle the top with grated cheddar cheese.
- **Bake:** Bake in a preheated oven for 25 minutes. Sprinkle the remaining French fried onions on top and bake for another 5-10 minutes or until bubbling and golden brown.
- **Serve:** Allow to cool slightly before serving.

Canned peach crisp.

Ingredients:

2 cans (15 oz.) of canned peaches in syrup, drained

1 cup rolled oats.

1/2 cup all-purpose flour.

1/2 cup packed brown sugar.

1/4 cup granulated sugar.

1/4 teaspoon of ground cinnamon.

1/4 teaspoon salt.

1/4 cup butter, melted

Instructions:

- **Preheat the Oven:** Preheat the oven to 350°F (175° C).
- **Prepare Filling:** Place the canned peaches in a baking dish. Sprinkle with granulated sugar if desired.
- **Make topping:** In a bowl, combine the oats, flour, brown sugar, cinnamon, and salt. Stir in the melted butter until crumbly.
- **Assemble:** Sprinkle the oat mixture evenly over the peaches.
- **Bake:** Bake for 30-35 minutes, until the topping is golden brown and the peach filling is bubbling.
- **Serve:** Serve warm, topped with vanilla ice cream or whipped cream.

Canned beef stew.

Ingredients:

2 cans (15 oz.) of tinned beef stew

1 cup frozen peas.

1 cup chopped carrots.

1 cup diced potatoes.

1 tablespoon of Worcestershire sauce.

1/2 teaspoon dried thyme.

Add salt and pepper to taste.

Instructions:

- **Combine Ingredients:** In a large pot, mix tinned beef stew, peas, carrots, potatoes, Worcestershire sauce, and thyme.
- **Simmer:** Heat over medium heat, stirring periodically, until the veggies are soft and the stew is thoroughly heated.
- **Adjust seasoning:** Taste and adjust seasoning with salt and pepper as needed.
- **Serve:** Serve hot alongside crusty bread or over rice.

These recipes make imaginative use of canned products, transforming them into delicious and satisfying dinners to suit a wide range of tastes and circumstances.

Gifting and Sharing Canned Foods

Presentation Ideas

- **Decorative Jars:** To make your canned products more festive, use jars with colorful lids or labels. To make them seem better, add ribbons, cloth covers, or custom labels.
- **Gift Baskets:** Make a themed gift basket using canned products like jams, pickles, and sauces. Include some complementary foods, such as crackers or cheese.
- **Holiday and Special Occasion Packaging:** For holidays or special occasions, consider including seasonal decorations or cards with your canned food gifts.

Labelling and Personalization

- **Custom Labels:** Create and print labels that include the contents, canning date, and any unique remarks. Include serving suggestions or recipes to give it a personalized touch.
- **Recipe Cards:** Attach recipe cards with ideas for how to use canned products. This is a useful handbook that adds a kind touch to your gift.

Considerations for Gifting

Consider the recipient's preferences and dietary constraints when choosing canned items. Customize your present to their tastes for a more personal touch.

- **Quality Assurance:** Before giving canned goods as a present, be sure they are in pristine shape. Check for indicators of deterioration or damage to ensure the recipient receives a high-quality good.

Sharing with the Community.

- **Food Drives and Charities:** Donate canned goods to your local food bank, shelter, or community kitchen. Canned meals are always in demand and can make a significant difference for people in need.
- **Potlucks & Gatherings:** Bring your handmade canned goods to potlucks or family gatherings. They look great on the table and let you show off your canning talents.

Seasonal and themed gifts.

- **Seasonal Gifts:** Choose canned items that represent the season, like as spicy apple butter for fall or refreshing fruit preserves for summer.
- **Themed Collections:** Make themed presents based on the recipient's preferences, such as a barbecue kit with homemade sauces and relishes or a breakfast basket with jams and jellies.

Safe handling and storage.

Check that all jars are correctly sealed and in good condition before giving. This prevents rotting and guarantees that the recipient receives safe and delicious food.

- **Storage instructions:** Provide storage instructions for your canned goods, including how to store them and any shelf-life concerns. This helps the recipient preserve the canned items in good shape.

Gifting and sharing canned foods can be a meaningful way to express joy while also providing people with homemade delicacies. By paying attention to presentation, personalization, and correct handling, you can make canned food presents unique and appreciated.

Crafting with Canning Jars

Candle Holders

Canning jars, candles or tea lights, and decorative things (e.g., glitter, ribbons, or paints).

Instructions:

Clean and dry the jars completely.

If desired, paint the outside of the jar or add ornamental accents.

Place a candle or tea light in the jar.

Tie a ribbon or string around the jar's neck to add some flair.

Flower Vases

Materials: Canning jars, flowers, and water.

Instructions: Clean the jar and remove labels.

Fill the jar with water, then place fresh flowers inside.

To achieve a rustic look, paint or wrap the jar in burlap or ribbon.

Storage containers

Materials include canning jars, labels, and pantry items.

Instructions:

Wash and dry the jars.

Label the jars with their contents and dates.

Jars are ideal for storing and organizing food items and craft supplies.

Terrariums

Canning jars, small plants or succulents, potting soil, ornamental stones, or gravel.

Instructions:

To facilitate drainage, layer gravel or stones at the bottom of the jar.

Add a layer of potting soil.

Plant your succulents and tiny plants.

If desired, decorate with more stones or moss.

Snow Globes

Materials: Canning jars, miniature plastic or ceramic figures, glitter, glycerin, water, and hot glue.

Instructions:

Attach the figurines to the interior of the jar lid with hot glue.

Fill the jar with water, then add a few drops of glycerin and glitter.

Screw the lid tightly to the jar.

Shake to generate the snow globe effect.

Personalized Drinking Glasses

Canning jars, straws, and paint or glass markers will be used.

Clean and dry the jars.

Decorate using paint or glass markers.

Use the jars as distinctive drink glasses at gatherings or daily.

Herb gardens

Ingredients: Canning jars, dirt, and herb seeds or seedlings.

Fill jars with potting soil.

Plant herbal seeds or seedlings.

Place in a sunny location and water regularly.

Party Favors

Materials include canning jars, chocolates, little trinkets, and ornamental objects.

Fill jars with party favors, such as sweets, tiny toys, or homemade snacks.

Decorate with ribbons, labels, or personalized tags.

Seal and serve as party favors.

Miniature Storage

Materials include miniature canning jars, beads, buttons, and other small crafts supplies.

Clean and dry the jars.

Jars are ideal for storing little goods such as beads, buttons, and craft supplies.

Label or decorate as needed for the organization.

Canning jars are adaptable and can be reused for a variety of artistic and practical applications. Whether for home decor, organization, or gifting, these ideas will help you get the most out of your jars beyond their typical uses.

Made in the USA
Coppell, TX
25 September 2024